THE COURTS GOVERNMENT AND HIGHER EDUCATION

Robert M. O'Neil

Vice President and Provost
for Academic Affairs
University of Cincinnati

DISCARD

Andrew S. Thomas Memorial Library
MORRIS HARVEY COLLEGE, CHARLESTON, W. VA.

COMMITTEE FOR ECONOMIC DEVELOPMENT

New York   Washington

379.12
On2c

The Committee for Economic Development is an independent research and educational organization of two hundred businessmen and educators. CED is nonprofit, nonpartisan, and nonpolitical and is supported by contributions from business, foundations, and individuals.

All CED policy recommendations must be approved by the Research and Policy Committee, a group of sixty trustees, which alone can speak for the organization. In issuing Statements on National Policy, CED often publishes background papers deemed worthy of wider circulation because of their contribution to the understanding of a public problem. This study relates to *Innovation in Education: New Directions for the American School* (1968) and other statements on education. It has been approved for publication as Supplementary Paper Number 37 by an editorial board of trustees and advisors. It also has been read by the members of the Research Advisory Board, who have the right to submit individual memoranda of comment for publication.

While publication of this supplementary paper is authorized by CED's bylaws, except as noted above its contents have not been approved, disapproved, or acted upon by the Committee for Economic Development, the Board of Trustees, the Research and Policy Committee, the Research Advisory Board, the research staff, or any member of any board or committee, or any officer of CED.

Copyright © 1972 by the Committee for Economic Development

All rights reserved. No part of this book may be reproduced or utilized in any form or by any means, electronic or mechanical, including photocopying, recording, or by any information storage or retrieval system, without permission in writing from the Committee for Economic Development.

Printed in the United States of America

Library of Congress Catalog Card Number: 72-90171

International Standard Book Number: 0-87186-237-9

Committee for Economic Development
477 Madison Avenue, New York, N.Y. 10022

THE COURTS GOVERNMENT AND HIGHER EDUCATION
Robert M. O'Neil

Several months after the Allende government came to power, the rector of the University of Chile was placed under indictment. The charge apparently pertained to a protest march from the campus to the presidential palace—a march the rector was said to have condoned. The demonstration grew out of a student strike supporting the rector in response to fears that Marxist and socialist students, who staged a sit-in at the rector's office, were trying to take over the hitherto autonomous university for political ends.

American college and university administrators doubtless have viewed events in Chile with some apprehension, but they have generally supposed that the rector's plight could not come to pass in the United States. In fact, however, their apprehension may be the more appropriate response.

Within weeks after the Kent-Cambodia crisis in the spring of 1970, a suit was brought against the chancellor of Washington University for $7.7 million; the student plaintiffs claimed that the relaxation of normal academic rules and the failure to call the police quickly enough during an anti-ROTC demonstration caused them to lose valuable classroom and extracurricular experience. Shortly thereafter a suit was filed in New York seeking to compel the commissioner of education to "punish" the president of State University College at Fredonia; the suit reflected an angry citizen's claim that the president had "permitted members of his staff and faculty to participate in a student strike." The trustees and administration of Indiana State University at Terre Haute were sued for $50,000 for failing to take prompt police action against a group of student demonstrators who damaged campus property in the early spring of 1970. Conservative student groups filed suits in Minnesota and Wisconsin seeking to impose personal liability against the governing boards and administrative officers for permitting the interruption of normal educational pursuits in the spring of 1970; both actions were recently dismissed.

Even the specter of criminal liability is not as remote as one might suppose. A grand jury in upstate New York returned a criminal indictment against Hobart and William Smith colleges in the closing days of 1970. The charge was that the colleges had "recklessly tolerated certain conduct constituting the offense of coercion"—a transgression for which fines up to $10,000 might have been levied, and for which the nation's oldest Episcopal college could conceivably have lost its charter. The gist of the indictment was that college officials allegedly failed (at five o'clock in the morning) to prevent students from interfering with a narcotics raid led by an undercover agent who had been posing as a Hobart undergraduate. The charges were eventually dismissed and the colleges were acquitted, but not without rather substantial tangible and intangible costs.

These recent incidents suggest that the plight of the Chilean rector is not so remote after all. Clearly the courts have entered a vastly different relationship with the campus from the entente that has prevailed throughout most of the history of American higher education. The catalytic force was neither the wave of student protest in the mid-1960s, nor the opening of the federal courts to the suits of suspended or dismissed students. What really effected this major realignment in court-campus relations was the flood of litigation after the Kent-Cambodia crisis in May 1970. Any assumptions about the future of law and higher education have been profoundly altered by these events.

HIGHER EDUCATION IN THE 1970s

This study considers several aspects of that relationship. It begins with a series of assumptions about the direction and character of American higher education during the 1970s, providing an essential backdrop for further analysis. It then develops a series of projections or predictions about the impact of law upon higher education. The paper concludes with a set of recommendations for the smoother adaptation of institutions of higher learning to the conditions projected.

Predictions about the future of higher education are always risky—as risky today as were the hopeful but naive claims during the 1960s that each year of campus disorder would be the last. The risks can be minimized to some degree, however, by making explicit the assumptions on which they rest. The articulation of such assumptions are also an acknowledgment of this writer's perspective, since no two lawyers or legal scholars would see the future in precisely the same way. The following assumptions are offered as a point of departure.

The current financial austerity will continue into the indefinite future, affecting both private and public campuses. Little need be said here about the current financial condition of higher education. Present trends suggest that the scarcity of resources will continue for the foreseeable future, income barely meeting or falling short of predictably rising costs. Not only are the demands of competing claimants for governmental funds likely to intensify during the 1970s, but higher education is unlikely soon to regain the high priority it held in the late 1950s and 1960s. On the one hand, legislators will not quickly forget the campus troubles of the recent past. Moreover, they have now learned that even eminent universities can survive despite curtailment of support. (At the University of California at Berkeley, for example, resignations of full professors ran about twenty-five a year during the era of rising budgets; in 1970–71, the first year of acute austerity, only twelve senior faculty members departed.)

Meanwhile, costs will presumably continue to rise. Development of new educational programs—especially those to improve the quality of undergraduate instruction—is likely to increase the costs. Only a sharp alteration in the character of American higher education would relieve the fiscal pressure—and no such change is predicted here. Minor alterations are foreseeable, such as, for example, increasing mergers of institutions and the sharing of expensive resources. Duplication and overlap in programs of nearby institutions will probably be reduced, and some low-demand programs will doubtless be eliminated. However, the resulting savings will not materially relieve the pressure.

Demands for governmental support of the private sector will increase and will be met. Despite the fiscal exigency of the public institutions, state and federal governments will be called upon to expand direct aid to the private sector. The number of states that have recently inaugurated such subvention programs is revealing; while New York's system of per capita grants to private institutions is still the largest, burgeoning programs and intensive studies in many states indicate the future course. With increased support will probably come increased governmental control and regulation of the private sector, mounting tension between once autonomous private campuses and state coordinating boards, and so forth. Finally, there will surely be continued competition between public and private institutions for scarce funds from both governmental and nongovernmental sources.

The development of comprehensive statewide systems will continue. Consolidation has proceeded apace in recent years and is likely to persist. The merger in 1971 of Wisconsin's two systems—each of which had been among the nation's largest—and the consolidation of all public campuses in North Carolina reflect the trend. Such mergers appear designed partly to anticipate collective bargaining, which offers "management" some advantages on a statewide basis, and partly to effect economies through uniformity and coordination. Often, too, there are special indigenous reasons for the fusion of once separate institutions, not the least of which is the impressive enrollment totals that result from combined data reporting.

The level of student activism and protest will decrease sharply and remain rather low through the 1970s. Student protest has stilled not so much because the issues have disappeared, but rather because the attitudes and expectations of students seem to have changed—those who are most alienated dropping out of the system altogether and those who might occasionally have joined protests against the system in the past now working within it. The downturn in the economy and the drastic shortage of employment opportunities (with or without graduate degrees) doubtless reinforce the current calm. A sharp revival of interest in academic pursuits appears to be either a cause or a result of the current condition; no one is quite sure which. In any case, the prognosis for the future seems relatively stable.

The level of faculty activism will increase and remain rather high during the 1970s. It may be an overstatement to say that the student demonstrators of the 1960s are becoming the junior faculty of the 1970s, but this is certainly part of the picture. Those who have the greatest distrust of administration and authority are entering the professoriat at precisely the time when the scarcity of resources gives them gravest cause for concern about their own status and their relations with senior colleagues. The advent of collective bargaining is likely to enhance the level of activism, as three major national groups vie for recognition, along with various local faculty organizations. The restructuring of campus governance, modest though it has been, affords junior faculty members new channels for expressing their concerns, raising expectations that the voices of a long-neglected constituency will at least be heeded. To the extent administrators respond to the pleas of the younger teachers, the senior faculty may feel slighted and may seek alternative ways of asserting and protecting their own interests. (Witness, for example, the response of the senior professors to the teaching assistants' strike at Wisconsin, and the initial creation at the City University of New York of two separate faculty unions, which have recently been merged.) While the activism of faculty is unlikely to reach the barricades save in extreme cases, the pressures will be far more intense than those of the past.

The demands for inclusion of historically excluded constituencies will continue to increase. Recent expansion of access—to employment, admissions, participation in university decision making—has created a revolution of rising expectations that cannot now be reversed. Minority groups are unlikely to accept the claim that 5 per cent black undergraduates is enough, nor will women be satisfied when the sex balance of faculties merely approximates the composition of graduate student bodies. Meanwhile, those who have been excluded from preferential programs designed to *benefit* minority groups are already beginning to demand comparable access; obviously not all groups can receive such preferences.

Apart from these historically neglected claimants, there are other groups to consider. The nonacademic staff and possibly even the emeriti will seek involvement in certain faculty-administration deliberations. The surrounding community, having passed by the campus gates for decades, will begin to claim a role in campus decision making. Students who have been admitted part way into institutional governance will seek more and broader avenues of access, including a stake in faculty promotion and tenure decisions. Such claims, moreover, will be increasingly legitimated. Whatever the motivation for Governor George Wallace's recent appointment of students to the University of Alabama board, this action suggests the extent of nonrevolutionary student participation at the highest level of governance.

Demands for participation will have to be accommodated within current structures since major reform seems unlikely. Despite the intense pressures for change, revisions in the structure and governance of American colleges and universities have been minimal. Adherence to traditional forms partly reflects the lack of suitable alternative models. Partly, too, it reflects the failure of scholars to devote to the study of their own institutions the skill and time that have been spent upon hospitals, corporations, government agencies, and countless other organizations. If major reform has not occurred before now, it is unlikely to occur in the future, given the conditions projected above. There is one corollary assumption: that even the widespread adoption of collective bargaining—should it come during the 1970s—would not effect major structural change, though the locus of decision making would doubtless be altered in some respects.

With these assumptions in mind, let us now consider the relations between law and higher education brought about by legislatures, courts, and various other external agencies. Of primary concern here are the autonomy and accountability of the administration of institutions of higher education as these institutions confront the law and the outside world.

LEGISLATURES AND CAMPUSES

Two years ago the executive director of the National Association of State Universities and Land-Grant Colleges remarked that legislators aroused by campus disorder "would intervene in a minute if only they knew what to do." Events since suggest that state lawmakers have learned precisely how to intervene and have few qualms about doing so. There are many instances of direct intervention. For example, rigid, formulistic, faculty workload conditions have been attached to university appropriations in New York, Michigan, Florida, and Washington; similar efforts have been narrowly defeated in Illinois, Arizona, and other states. There are special punitive statutes, adopted in some form by the legislatures of thirty-two states during 1969–70. Particular examples merit brief comment: i.e., the Pennsylvania law that required colleges and universities throughout the world to report certain transgressions of Pennsylvania students as the condition of eligibility for state loans or scholarships, and the Ohio statute that authorized suspension of a student, faculty, or staff member following arrest for a wide range of offenses and mandated dismissal upon conviction. This is not the place to detail the provisions of such legislation, but simply to illustrate the pattern.

Legislatures have recently intervened in a variety of other ways. After the close of the regular 1971 session, the presiding officers of the two houses and the chairmen of the two education committees of the Minnesota legislature sent letters to each campus president setting forth a list of "particulars" to guide the disbursement of the appropriated funds—advice that would be disregarded at peril, even though it lacked the concurrence of either house or the approval of the governor. Legislatures may intervene through budgetary deletion as much as through affirmative regulation—as, for example, when California eliminated funds for faculty salary increases and for the academic senate in 1970, or when New York abolished sabbatical leaves.

Legislative inquiry or surveillance also has profound implications for campus governance and autonomy. During the summer following the May 1970 Kent-Cambodia crisis, formal investigations were launched—notably in Ohio, Illinois, Indiana, and Virginia. In announcing the Illinois inquiry, the chairman of the special state senate investigating committee told the press his key concern: "We want no Angela Davises in Illinois." His counterpart in Virginia announced the committee's desire to assure the taxpayers that "their funds are not being squandered by students who do not study and teachers who do not teach." Six months later, the New York Office of Legislative Research (at lawmakers' request) asked the presidents of more than thirty State University of New York campuses for detailed information about various courses in the social sciences. The target of the inquiry was courses dealing with "revolution," "the Establishment," sociology, and urban studies, with particular attention to the "instructor's orientation."

There is a common theme running through these rather novel forms of legislative intervention. While surveillance and accountability are of course appropriate when an elected body allocates millions of dollars for the support of higher education, such actions and inquiries as these exceed the legitimate needs of oversight. They tend to substitute inexpert (sometimes politically motivated) judgment about such matters as faculty workload, faculty and student discipline, and academic leaves for the experienced and responsible judgment of governing boards and administrators. Indeed, the invasion of the autonomy of the regents or trustees by such actions may be even graver than the displacement of administrative initiative, since legally the governing board holds all ultimate authority.

Private institutions can also expect increasing control as they become progressively dependent upon the public purse. In New York, for example, the Board of Regents has held broad regulatory power over private educational institutions since colonial times. The power has been infrequently invoked, however, save in the approval of new degrees and degree programs. Recently the regents proposed a comprehensive "master plan" for joint development of public and private campuses in the New York City metropolitan area. A key ingredient would be the consolidation of "relatively expensive graduate and professional programs in fields of limited enrollment," and a study of the role of the private institutions in "helping to implement the City

University's open admissions program." There is at least the subtle hint that state support of the private sector may in the future reflect the extent of cooperation with the public sector.

That prospect derives credence from the posture of the New York legislature toward the private campuses. In the summer of 1970 the so-called Henderson law was enacted, requiring all colleges and universities chartered by the regents to adopt and file student conduct regulations and disciplinary procedures. An institution which failed to comply would become ineligible for "any state aid or assistance." Given the growing importance to the private campuses of the per capita payments authorized by the legislature to private colleges and universities following the recommendations of the 1968 Bundy Commission report, it is readily understandable that few institutions failed to file.

While New York is more advanced in this regard, it is not alone. Several state legislatures, in the wake of the Kent-Cambodia crisis, enacted laws forbidding firearms at all institutions of higher learning. Massachusetts some years ago sought to impose a loyalty oath on faculty members at private institutions. The Pennsylvania scholarship law cited earlier required private as well as public colleges to report student violations as a condition of continuing eligibility. Recently New Jersey has unveiled a new plan for direct aid to private universities, contingent upon a commitment "to educate more New Jersey students, with particular emphasis on students from low-income families." Given the likelihood of continued scarcity of resources for higher education, the expansion of state regulation and control of the private sector seems a probable condition of continued subvention.

Legislative intrusion of various forms will probably continue into the foreseeable future—well beyond the catalytic period of student unrest—for several reasons. First, the scarcity of funds and the change in the academic marketplace gives the legislatures substantially stronger leverage over the campuses than existed in the highly competitive 1960s. The rapid rise of competing claims within a relatively static state budget increases both the apparent needs and justification for tighter control of university expenditures. Second, both the lawmakers and their committee staffs have become far more sophisticated about the internal workings of colleges and universities as a result of the Kent-Cambodia aftermath. Since they do "know how to intervene" they are far less likely to defer to claims of institutional or governing board autonomy than was typical in the past. Third, the development of statewide coordination and control is likely to intensify legislative activity in any event. Finally, the mere fact of having taken the first step with impunity may embolden lawmakers who were once timid or deferential toward university trustees and presidents. Thus, in the absence of a major change in the availability of resources or in the climate of public opinion, continued legislative intrusion seems predictable.

Such action is bound, however, to evoke a reaction. The Michigan legislature attached a spate of conditions to the 1970 budget appropriation, including detailed prescriptions for faculty staffing formulas and workloads, tuition rates and waivers, student and faculty conduct, resident-nonresident student ratios, and other matters once thought the province of the trustees and the campus administrations. Instead of accepting the restrictions, the governing boards of the University of Michigan, Michigan State University, and Wayne State University decided to fight. They brought suit in the state courts contending that such conditions violated the constitutional autonomy of the three boards. In December 1971, the court ruled in the universities' favor on most of the conditions, holding that the legislature had exceeded its constitutional powers and abridged those of another branch of government.*

A composite prediction now emerges: regardless of the level or recurrence of student protest, legislative regulation of academic life is likely to persist up to the point it is checked by the courts. All factors seem to point toward continued regulation as well as continued oversight. As these pressures intensify, the need for protective measures will increase correspondingly. In some states this may take the form of litigation on the Michigan model. There are other states, however, where the courts simply will not accept suits by a state agency challenging legislation under which it operates. (For this reason the Colorado courts refused for several years to hear a challenge by the regents to the constitutionality of a faculty loyalty oath which the board was required to impose.) In other states, the defense of academic autonomy may require lobbying—of the kind that was strikingly effective in warding off proposed faculty workload conditions in Illinois and Ohio. Where the university is merely a creature of statute, constitutional amendment may be the answer—just as the California Constitutional Revision Commission now proposes constitutional status for the trustees of the state colleges. Finally, greater reliance on alternative sources of funds may afford the solution that is soundest, if the most difficult to achieve. The

---

* Neither the suit nor the decision is unprecedented. There has been a history of protective litigation in Michigan. The university regents sued the legislature in 1911 to vindicate their autonomy in the use of appropriated funds; the Michigan State University board did the same three years later. Surprisingly, the Michigan experience does not seem to have been followed elsewhere, though in a dozen other states—California among them—the universities similarly enjoy constitutional stature.

experience of what might be called semi-state universities has been rather mixed; Rutgers is perhaps more extensively and closely regulated than almost any pure state-supported institution, while the universities of Vermont, Pittsburgh, and Cincinnati seem to have derived a measure of independence from the duality of their financial bases. The long-range solution may lie in diversification of support more than in any of the other, essentially short-range options outlined here. For the moment it is quite unclear how feasible that solution will be.

COURTS AND CAMPUSES

The legislatures have not been alone in challenging campus autonomy. Judicial intervention also poses a significant threat, as witness the several aforementioned suits brought against campus administrators and governing boards as a result of campus disorder. All but one of the cases noted were ultimately dismissed—but not without considerable costs in legal fees, time and energy, and a virtually certain chilling effect upon future administrative behavior. There is other disquieting evidence of the rapid increase in the litigation of campus issues.

As has been noted, the Kent-Cambodia period was the watershed. Most dramatic was the use of the courts to open or close an entire campus during the critical days of May—a court in Ohio ordered the Kent State campus closed indefinitely, while a judge in Florida ordered the University of Miami to reopen after closing down the day following the Kent tragedy. Later came the wave of damage suits—the cases involving alleged administrative malfeasance at Washington University, Indiana State University, the state universities of Wisconsin and Minnesota, and others which have already been cited.

Nowhere was the range of litigated issues broader than in New York. The Court of Appeals decided, against the pleas of law faculties, that students would be eligible to take the 1970 summer bar examination only after completing "regular, written examinations" in all their courses—though many classes had already been dismissed for the year. A small claims court held New York University accountable for $277.40, a pro rata share of tuition and fees representing instruction "lost" as a result of the early closing recommended by the University Senate. (The judgment was eventually overturned by an appellate court, which ruled that the small claims judge "erred in substituting [his] judgment for that of the university administrators and in concluding that the university was unjustified in suspending classes or the time remaining in the school year prior to the examination period.")

Perhaps the most dramatic action of a New York court involved a suit brought by a group of Queens College students soon after its closing at the time of the Cambodian crisis, claiming they had been unlawfully denied instruction in certain specific courses. The suit was partly based on a May 10 resolution of the Board of Higher Education requiring all units of the City University of New York (CUNY) to "remain open to continue to offer instruction to the students. . . ." The resolution also provided that "colleges may adjust their programs of courses, attendance, examinations and grading as in their judgment may seem necessary and appropriate." Yet the court held in the plaintiffs' favor and ordered the Queens faculty to provide special instruction in the designated subjects. Thus the court found no latitude for individual adjustment to the end-of-the-year crisis—even though the governing board had delegated substantial discretion to each campus and its faculty.

In other cases New York courts have been used to keep a college president in office (against the order of the governing board), and to bar a president-designate from taking office (at the behest of student leaders not consulted in the selection). Judges have on several occasions ordered the awarding of degrees denied by campus officials—not merely because of claims of discriminatory or improper evaluation of student work but on the basis of an independent appraisal of a student record. Another court recently held that the legislature meant to eliminate sabbatical leaves for City University faculty, even though the law expressly exempted prior contractual arrangements—a proviso apparently intended to cover CUNY's collective bargaining agreement. And so it goes, through a rapidly lengthening list of campus issues. There hardly seems to be a question too sensitive or too complex to find its way into the New York courts.*

While the New York experience may be extreme, it differs only in degree from the national pattern. Within the past two or three years the federal courts have become forums for the litigation of a broad range of issues that one would not have thought justiciable a decade ago: legality of dormitory room searches; confidentiality of student files and records of student organizations; recognition and status of student political groups; administrative control over campus newspapers and other publications; access of insiders and outsiders to campus facilities for meetings and rallies; denial of enrollment in or credit for particular courses as well as degree programs; withdrawal of student government positions or offices from alleged campus wrongdoers; and other com-

---

* There is a special factor in New York: Article 78 of the Code of Civil Procedure makes the acts and decisions of private as well as public colleges and universities more readily reviewable in court than is the case in most other states.

parable issues. Nor were the issues noted in this list approached lightly; while the majority of cases went against the plaintiffs, a surprising number held that the university had abridged constitutional liberties of students, faculty or staff members, or of outsiders seeking access to the campus.

Until the summer of 1972, most law affecting colleges and universities was made by state and lower federal courts. Incredible as it seems, for nearly forty years the United States Supreme Court did not review and decide on the merits of a single case involving college-student rights. (The last such case was in 1934, when the court held that the University of California could constitutionally require all male students to take part in ROTC.) In mid-1972 there were two decisions of the first importance—one involving constitutional rights of student organizations seeking campus recognition and the other involving constitutional claims of nontenured faculty faced with termination.

The first case arose in the federal courts when the president of Central Connecticut State College refused recognition to a campus chapter of Students for a Democratic Society (SDS). When the students went initially to court, the judge ordered a hearing on the campus, which was promptly held. The decision was still adverse to the organization's claim, the administration maintaining that SDS would be a "disruptive influence" on the campus and that recognition would be "contrary to the orderly process of change" at the college. The lower federal courts sustained this judgment and the SDS petition eventually reached the Supreme Court.

A unanimous Court, including all of President Nixon's appointees, held that the college had violated rights of the students and student group in refusing recognition. The decision began by establishing a vital and much-debated proposition: "The precedents of this Court leave no room for the view that, because of the acknowledged need for order, First Amendment protections should apply with less force on college campuses than in the community at large." The implications of this precept were apparent for the immediate case. The lower courts had improperly discounted constitutional claims to freedom of expression and association of the students—claims that were asserted through the SDS chapter for which they sought recognition. Moreover, the lower courts had unconstitutionally placed upon the students the burden of proving they were entitled to recognition, rather than requiring the college to show that nonrecognition was warranted. Once the students had made application for recognition through the procedures of the college, and had met the formal or technical requirements, then the burden shifted to the administration. Finally, the Court concluded that the judgment of the college administration did in fact abridge First Amendment freedoms to the extent it rested upon an assumed relationship between the local and national SDS groups, or anticipated probable violence or disruption, since the record contained no proof that such results would follow. There was one matter left unclear by the lower court hearings, however. Recognition might have been denied if the group had, in fact, failed to comply with a rule requiring them to abide by reasonable campus regulations. To gain additional information on that point, the justices remanded the case to the district court for further proceedings.

Later in the same week, a sharply divided Supreme Court announced equally important principles affecting rights of nontenured faculty. Two cases (among dozens decided by lower courts since 1970) reached the Court about the same time, both involving nontenured faculty members who had been denied reappointment without explanation or an opportunity for a hearing. In both cases the faculty members claimed that constitutional rights had been breached because of the absence of procedures within the college. In both instances the lower federal courts agreed with the professors' constitutional claims.

On the basic question, six justices agreed that the federal Constitution does not require an opportunity for a hearing prior to the nonrenewal of a probationary teacher's contract, unless the teacher can show that the nonrenewal deprived him of an interest in "liberty" or that he had a "property" interest in continued employment by the institution. In one of the two cases, the majority went on to find that no constitutional rights had been denied because there was no proof that the nonrenewal either imposed a stigma or was tantamount to a deprivation of personal liberty. Nor did the terms and conditions of the professor's one year contract at the college give him a property interest in continuing employment that would entitle him to a hearing under recent Supreme Court decisions dealing with rights of welfare recipients and other beneficiaries.

In the other case, however, the faculty member had made a strong claim that he was terminated because of the exercise of his rights of free speech. Here the Court held that the district judge had improperly foreclosed consideration of the question whether the nonrenewal decision was based on the exercise of First Amendment rights, which would have been unconstitutional. Moreover, the policies of the college in the second case may have created a kind of de facto tenure. While the college officially did not recognize or confer tenure on its faculty, the Court felt that the terms and circumstances of employment created a sufficient expectancy that a hearing should be held at which the faculty member could be informed of the reasons for his nonretention and could challenge the validity of those reasons.

The net effect of these two decisions is to require close scrutiny of the facts of each case involving a nontenured professor. In the absence of any special circumstances, the Constitution neither creates tenure of employment nor requires a hearing. But particular cases may contain various elements that will require procedures not generally accorded by the college. Where the effect of the termination is to create some sort of stigma, or where the faculty member alleges an infringement of First Amendment rights, it now appears that a statement of reasons should be given and an opportunity afforded for a campus hearing. Clearly this is the case where the terms and conditions of employment create a reasonable expectancy of continued employment—the kind of "de facto tenure" the Court perceived in the second case. It is less clear what procedures are required where a stigma or First Amendment claim is involved but there is no property kind of job security at stake. Doubtless it will take some time before the lower courts have a chance to work out the full implications of these profoundly important decisions.

Against this complex background, predictions for the future are hazardous. Many issues remain unresolved—either because they have not been litigated at all or because the decisions to date are in conflict at the trial court level. In these and other areas, increasing resort to the courts seems likely for a number of reasons.

First, student plaintiffs have achieved a remarkably high rate of success in cases brought since the federal courts were opened to their constitutional claims in 1961. Thus the incentive to continue challenging university policy in this forum remains strong despite occasional setbacks.

Second, the availability of legal services continues to increase. A growing number of student governments and campus organizations have retained attorneys or law firms on an essentially open-ended basis, in somewhat the same fashion as have the labor-union legal-service plans that have recently been held by the Supreme Court to be constitutionally protected. When distributed among a student body of 25,000 to 35,000, the costs of such a retainer are rather small and are often thought to be justified by a couple of major court victories a year. Administrators are by no means always opposed to such arrangements. Officials on the first campus to have such a formal retainer were initially hostile, but soon found dealing with the students' attorney easier and pleasanter than confronting the angry students themselves over every grievance.

Third, the courts have experienced somewhat the same leveling process as that affecting the legislatures. The once formidable and remote university president has now been a party defendant, a witness, and an affiant in enough cases to dispel some of the mystique. Courts still occasionally view the internal academic processes with awe and deference, but to many judges, especially the younger ones, there is nothing sacrosanct about a university as defendant. (Even the University of California, once the object of greatest judicial reverence, has now been held accountable to a medical student who claimed he was prevented from entering his fourth year because of the whim or malice of medical center officials and teachers.)

Fourth, the courts are likely to become more rather than less accessible to aggrieved members of the academic communities. Already in several states administrative procedure statutes make campus actions (and sometimes inactions) subject to court review in the manner of ordinary administrative agency proceedings. The tendency has been to expand the applicability of such laws; recently the Washington legislature expressly included the university (as Oregon did some years earlier); and the courts have recently effected the same result in Maryland.

Increased access to courts is not inevitable, however. California, where the administrative procedure act is inapplicable to institutions of higher learning, has recently discouraged such litigation. In 1967 the legislature required all plaintiffs suing the regents of the University of California to post security to meet the litigation costs ($100 per plaintiff or more if the court deemed it necessary). The law also provides that the costs are to be borne by the plaintiffs if they lose the case. Should other states erect comparable barriers to the litigation of academic grievances, the trends projected here would doubtless be altered—though at considerable cost to those who are legitimately aggrieved and need the aid of an impartial tribunal.

Substantively, it is probable that courts will insist on stronger evidence of some special university interest as the basis for discipline or sanction. That is, the academic community may not punish its members simply because they have broken the law, but only when the conduct in question has impaired some special concern of an academic institution. A distinction will increasingly be drawn between two types of transgressions—equally unlawful in the criminal courts—the one involving a member of the campus community and the other involving persons unrelated to the campus. Thus different treatment may be appropriate for stealing a book from the bookstore, and stealing a reserve book from the university library; for provoking a fist fight in the classroom, and doing the same thing in a bar; for committing perjury while studying law, and committing the same offense while pursuing a chemistry major. These distinctions are subtle, but vital, in relation to the progressive refinement of campus law. A few courts have already drawn attention to them, although no decision turns dispositively on the presence or absence of affected university interests.

Finally, the volume of academic litigation will depend most of all upon the extent to which colleges and universities maintain order in their own houses. Many court decisions reveal a substantial and appropriate degree of deference to internal due process. One reason why the University of California has fared so well in the courts seems to be the extent to which campus procedural rules have anticipated the judicial decree. Even on the question of whether activist law student Dan Siegel could be suspended from his student government office for his role in the People's Park demonstration in 1969, the Berkeley campus administration insisted on a full and formal hearing. When Siegel sued in federal court to regain his position, the judgment against him clearly reflected a belief that Siegel had received all process he was due.

EQUALITY IN THE ALLOCATION OF BENEFITS AND OPPORTUNITIES

The issue of equality clearly warrants a separate paper of its own and can receive only the briefest treatment here. Looking ahead through the 1970s, it seems probable that courts, legislatures, and some administrative agencies will insist that departures from neutrality in matters of employment, admissions, financial aids, and academic evaluation be justified by a close relationship to some legitimate university interest. Most clearly this precept applies to discrimination against racial and ethnic minority groups, and less obviously (though almost inevitably) to preferential discrimination and compensatory programs. At the further reaches of equality there are the questions of differing standards for men and women and for resident and nonresident students. All such differentials will receive increasing scrutiny in the coming decade.

The issue of segregated dual systems of public higher education has been a sensitive and difficult one because it implicates the whole future of the predominantly black colleges. The issue is not confined to the southern states, since traditionally black public campuses exist in Ohio, Pennsylvania, and Missouri. In addition, most large metropolitan areas now have two-year colleges with heavy minority enrollments, such as Laney, Compton, and Merritt in California; Malcolm X in Chicago; Bronx Community and others in New York City; there are even a few four-year campuses, e.g., Federal City College in the District of Columbia. Despite the complexity of the issue, the courts will have reached it, just as they have done much earlier in elementary and secondary education. A few cases have already reviewed the status of the dual collegiate systems. Most recently, a three-judge federal court in Virginia held that the state could not constitutionally upgrade a two-year white college to four-year status since that step would frustrate attempts to desegregate the neighboring black state college. Similar decisions have been rendered by federal courts in Alabama and Tennessee, though the evidence of compliance is still limited.

If the problem of segregation is analytically simple, the same cannot be said for the legal status of preferential and compensatory programs for minority groups. There has been much discussion of the constitutionality of such programs but, until very recently, no litigation. A case currently pending in the Supreme Court of Washington squarely presents the issue, however: a white Anglo student was denied admission to the Law School of the University of Washington while black and chicano applicants with lower grade point averages and test scores were accepted. Strictly on the basis of that differential, the Washington trial court held that unconstitutional discrimination had occurred and that the plaintiff was entitled to be enrolled. (There is in fact some doubt about the validity of that conclusion, since the particular plaintiff was fairly far down the "waiting list" and probably would never have been accepted even with no minority students in the picture. But the court nonetheless reached the constitutional claim.)

The validity of such preferential programs will presumably depend upon demonstration of educationally sound reasons for varying the traditional admissions criteria. Such reasons might include doubts about the reliability and fairness of the standard performance predictors, even for white Anglo students, and all the more so for minority applicants. The university's desire to overcome the effects of past overt discrimination against and exclusion of minorities might also be pertinent. A professional judgment that student bodies should be ethnically more reflective of the national population would also be persuasive. The university may assert, in support of its preferential program, a desire to prepare minority persons for essential community and public service roles that whites simply cannot perform. The points, then, are fairly simple. On the one hand, it will not do for the university to assert a merely altruistic desire to help minority persons. On the other hand, it will not do for courts to invoke the black letter principle that the Constitution is color blind. Clearly there must be some accommodation between the basic commitment to *neutrality* in educational administration and the urgent need to *equalize* opportunities that have long been denied to certain groups.

An important corollary follows this analysis. A vital difference must be recognized between *quotas* and *goals* in the attempt to increase opportunities for minority groups. Much of the criticism—that of Vice President Agnew, for example—confuses declarations of university commitment with setting of rigid percentage quotas to be filled regardless of the available pool of applicants. Recent court decisions reflect the distinction quite clearly. One federal court of appeals has sustained the constitutionality of the federal government's Philadelphia Plan, which determines percentage-range goals for minority employment on federal contracts. Another federal appellate court has held unconstitutional an order to hire without regard to relative qualifications the next twenty black persons who sought employment in a municipal fire department. The goal or range is probably valid if justified in terms of legitimate and substantial need; the quota or fixed percentage is probably invalid whatever the justification. Universities can be guided by such decisions as these.

Third, the question of sex-based discrimination will undoubtedly come under review, not only within the U.S. Department of Health, Education, and Welfare (HEW)—of which more later—but equally in the courts. Many forms of sex discrimination are still prevalent: public campuses in several states segregated by sex; higher admission standards for women than men at many institutions (defended by the claim that women would greatly outnumber men if parity were observed); shockingly low percentages of women in the higher faculty ranks at most campuses; and clear salary differentials at many institutions. There are subtler forms of discrimination as well—admission standards that look fair but in fact favor men because of weighting formulas; reduced financial aids for women students; limited options for participation of women in campus governance; and policies that fail to accommodate women's family and professional needs. The range of issues, in fact, is vast and just beginning to be made apparent to the academic community. (For an explanation of the precise concern of HEW, see page 22.)

As in the case of universities, the courts are just beginning to be aware of sex discrimination. Within recent years the Supreme Court had held that women could be barred from jury service and could be denied certain forms of employment on the basis of a merely "rational relationship" to some plausible state interest. A number of decisions have begun to question this formula. In the late fall of 1971 the Supreme Court struck down an Idaho law requiring a preference for men over women in the administration of a decedent's estate, regardless of experience, competence, or other factors. The California Supreme Court earlier in the year held unconstitutional a state law forbidding women to tend bar except in premises owned by them or a male relative. The California court, moreover, announced a fundamentally new standard for judging sex discrimination—essentially the "compelling interest" test the Supreme Court has applied to discrimination affecting other vital rights and liberties. So many cases are already in the courts that the California test is bound to be followed elsewhere, even though the United States Supreme Court felt no need to announce a stricter standard in the Idaho probate case.

Finally, there is the troublesome matter of discrimination based on place of residence. Countless student suits have challenged resident-nonresident tuition differentials, uniformly without success. The Supreme Court has not spoken directly on the issue, but recently did affirm without opinion a judgment sustaining Minnesota's resident-nonresident fee differential. Other forms of geographical discrimination may be even more vulnerable though they have not been as often tested. Increasing numbers of states have set percentage limits on nonresident enrollments. Perhaps the most extreme barrier was that adopted by Purdue University in 1969—an over-all nonresident quota of 25 per cent, additionally limiting the percentage of New York and New Jersey students to the national population proportion of those two states. Deep concern was expressed by the Anti-Defamation League, fearing that "such a policy, aimed at a major Jewish population center, imposed a special disability upon Jewish students interested in studying at Purdue." Whatever the motivation for this special regional restriction, Purdue modified the policy the following year.*

The whole matter of nonresident tuition has been greatly complicated by the recent legislation lowering the voting age to eighteen. Students have sought to register as voters in the communities where they attend college, regardless of their place of family residence. About two-thirds of the states have permitted such local registration. In one early case, a Kansas trial court held that a student who registers to vote in a college town is no longer subject to nonresident tuition and fees, but is to be considered a "resident" for all purposes. That decision has been appealed to the Kansas Supreme Court. A federal court in Connecticut

---

* The Anti-Defamation League has argued in a recent study that most nonresident restrictions, despite their apparent ethnic neutrality, subtly discriminate against Jews because of the higher proportion of Jewish students among nonresidents at many large state universities outside the Northeast. This allegation underscores the need to look for covert discrimination—even unintended discrimination—in seemingly innocuous admission policies.

reached a similar conclusion several months later. If these trial court judgments are upheld and followed in other states, virtually all students over eighteen could become instant residents of their college communities and render the nonresident classification meaningless in practice, even if still constitutionally valid in theory.

It is difficult to make comprehensive predictions covering these discrete forms of differentials. To venture a bit of oversimplification, the pattern may look like this over the next decade: racially-segregated systems of higher education, and probably sex-segregated systems, will almost certainly have to be integrated, either because HEW or the courts require it. Other forms of sex-based discrimination in admissions and employment will be challenged increasingly in the courts, the results depending on how the courts deal with other problems of sex-based discrimination. Preferential and compensatory admission policies and programs for minority students will be sustained to the extent they reflect substantial and legitimate educational interests; the demands of excluded groups will bring the constitutionality of such policies increasingly before the courts, whatever the outcome of the pending Washington case. Finally, nonresident tuition and fee differentials will be increasingly challenged, and rigid percentage limits on out-of-state students may fare less well in the courts. In short, some departures from neutrality will be allowed, to the extent they serve legitimate academic needs, while other departures will almost certainly be enjoined.

EXPANDING ROLE OF OTHER AGENCIES IN UNIVERSITY AFFAIRS

A brief review of recent events shows how broad is the range of administrative agencies potentially impinging upon university autonomy. The National Collegiate Athletic Association (NCAA) has long determined—with the feared power of exclusion from intercollegiate competition—a wide variety of academic and athletic policies. Admissions standards, scholarship and financial aid practices, and athletic department policies are potentially subject to extensive regulation. In the fall of 1971, for example, the NCAA declared the University of California at Berkeley ineligible for the football season because, through administrative oversight, two varsity players had failed to take a certain prefreshman examination. Both had respectable academic records and were in good standing, but that was irrelevant; having failed to take the test originally they could never thereafter be redeemed.

The regional accrediting associations, too, have a wider jurisdiction than is often realized. New academic programs and (especially in new institutions) novel structures and governance forms are sometimes foregone because of fear that accreditation may be jeopardized. Given the importance of membership in a regional association—affecting eligibility for most federal funds, acceptability of transfer credits, among others—it is hardly surprising that this matter is taken seriously. In some fields the greater threat may come from the *professional* accrediting groups rather than from the general regional associations; in disciplines such as engineering, the pressures toward conformity can be substantial. The strength of the professional association may also be a blessing, however. Threatened violations of academic freedom have occasionally been averted by a sharp warning from the accreditors, or an informal investigation where the warning did not suffice. These groups may also play a useful supporting role in fighting punitive legislation such as faculty workload formulas which, if applied to some professional fields, would jeopardize accreditation.

The National Labor Relations Board (NLRB) has also recently become involved in higher education. In the early 1950s the board declined to assert jurisdiction over private colleges and universities (the basic federal legislation has always placed public institutions of higher learning beyond the board's reach). Suddenly in the summer of 1970, NLRB reversed itself announcing that henceforth it would determine bargaining units and supervise elections on some private campuses. Several months later, this jurisdiction was defined in terms of annual receipts of at least $1 million—thus bringing nearly all private colleges and universities within the board's purview. A number of proceedings have since been held on private campuses, and NLRB agents have conducted and certified several faculty elections.

The assumption of NLRB jurisdiction over the private sector threatened another form of intervention. A board trial examiner startled the academic community by ordering Lawrence (Michigan) Institute of Technology to reinstate three nontenure faculty members found to have been terminated because of activities in the American Association of University Professors (AAUP). The board soon reversed the trial examiner's decision and thus withdrew temporarily from this sensitive arena. Some state labor boards and agencies, however, have handled similar complaints;* the very first case referred by New York's

---

* Recently the California Fair Employment Practices Commission for the first time ordered an academic institution (Fresno State College) to reinstate a faculty member after finding that his dismissal was motivated by racial bias. (A simultaneous appeal to the federal courts was unavailing.)

Public Employment Relations Board to a hearing officer involved a faculty member at a four-year college of the State University of New York (SUNY).

The Internal Revenue Service (IRS) frequently acts in ways that affect academic policy. Notably, the IRS position with regard to released time for political activity in the fall of 1970 (worked out with the American Council on Education) had a profound effect on the thinking of all tax-exempt colleges and universities—and would have had a much greater effect had the political momentum not been spent by fall. The tax status of campus publications has also been drawn in question by the IRS; a protracted proceeding involving the Columbia *Spectator* served warning that editorial endorsement of political candidates might jeopardize a needed tax exemption. (IRS ultimately restored the exemption, but the infraction had been relatively minor in scope and nonpartisan in character.)

Even the Federal Trade Commission (FTC) has recently entered the picture. A correspondence law school in Chicago was required by the commission to indicate clearly in its national advertising that its law courses do not qualify a student to take the bar examination in any state. An air career school on Long Island was recently ordered to refund tuition to a student who had taken seriously but unsuccessfully the school's claim that "if you are accepted you may rest easy about your future in the fascinating airlines field." Most academic institutions would not make such claims, of course; the decision nonetheless may serve warning to highly competitive admissions officers and to facile academic publicists.

The greatest current concern about administrative agency review of academic decisions comes in the area of affirmative action for women and minority groups. As a result of recent legislation, college and university personnel policies and decisions have come under review by the Department of Health, Education, and Welfare (through its Office for Civil Rights); the Department of Labor; and the Equal Employment Opportunity Commission. As originally enacted, the employment provisions of the Civil Rights Act of 1964 exempted the educational aspects of colleges and universities. But an amendment in the spring of 1972 removed the exemption, so that institutions of higher learning are now subject to essentially the same scrutiny as industrial and commercial employers.

Armed only with the nondiscrimination provisions of Title VI (federal funding) of the 1964 Civil Rights Act, HEW held up for some months the payment of contract funds to Columbia University and the University of Michigan, pending receipt of satisfactory affirmative action commitments. Notice has now been served that "goals and timetables" evidencing viable affirmative action programs will be expected from virtually all institutions of higher learning. Meanwhile, the HEW Office for Civil Rights has detailed guidelines for use of college and university administrators in developing and implementing affirmative action programs. In addition, aggrieved minority or women faculty members (as well as nonacademic personnel) may take complaints to the Equal Employment Opportunity Commission. The commission is charged initially to seek informal resolution or accommodation of any such complaint. If informal methods fail, the commission may then bring suit against an allegedly discriminatory employer. Following an adverse ruling by the commission, the aggrieved individual may also bring suit, and a court may be able to award up to two years' back pay following a finding of discrimination.

Affirmative action compliance proceedings may pose serious practical and operational problems for institutions of higher learning. Government officials may seek personnel and employment data which the administration would ordinarily deem confidential and would withhold from all external review. Procedures for review of alleged noncompliance have not yet been worked out fully, and some uncertainty remains whether due process will be fully ensured. Moreover, the time requirements for institutional responses to various stages in the proceeding are quite short, and some colleges have claimed they simply cannot complete the required tasks within the specified time.

In addition to the expanding scope of agency activity, other forces are tending toward displacement of internal university decision making. Reference has already been made to the 1970 Ohio law that authorizes suspension of a student, faculty, or staff member arrested for any of a rather long list of offenses. The decision of whether or not to suspend is to be made by a referee, an attorney not connected with the university and appointed by the regents. Thereafter, a conviction requires the automatic dismissal of the accused, with no further inquiry into his academic competence or status. Thus decisions at two levels are taken away from the internal experts and committed to a referee and a criminal jury.

The trustees of the California state colleges have recently adopted a new procedure, entrusting faculty dismissal cases to a professional external hearing examiner. Provision is made for review by a statewide faculty committee, so the professional academic judgment does play a potential role in such cases. But its redeeming importance is diluted in practice; the faculty committee must make a decision and report to the chancellor within *five* working days of the time it receives the findings. Thus the vital factual determinations are all made by an outsider, and the critical inferences may be left by default to the central administration and the trustees.

A recent court case reveals increasing resort to external decision makers in academic disputes. When a nontenured faculty member at Youngstown (Ohio) State University brought suit in federal court, claiming he had been denied due process by a decision not to renew his contract, the district judge assigned the case to a hearing officer, a Cleveland attorney. The hearing was held on the campus, but under the authority of the court—presumably including, for example, the power of subpoena. Thereafter, the judge simply adopted the hearing examiner's report and conclusions, adding a brief explanatory paragraph of his own. The use of special masters, referees, and the like is not new to the federal courts, of course, but is wholly novel in the treatment of academic issues.

Predicting the future of administrative displacement of campus decision making is harder than the projections made in other areas. Each of the sources of displacement examined here has a distinct concern. All agencies except the NCAA and the accrediting associations have come quite recently to the campus and are still feeling their way about in an unfamiliar world. Their inclination to remain on campus will depend upon various factors—the political pressures to which they are subjected; the relative importance of other responsibilities and assignments; agency manpower and resources; and the limitations imposed by reviewing courts. Perhaps most significant will be the response of the academic community itself to such threats. It is still too early to measure the strength of the will to resist, since even the nature of the threat is not fully appreciated.

LITIGATION OVER PARTICIPATION IN UNIVERSITY DECISION MAKING

Mentioned earlier was the revolution of rising expectations precipitated by partial inclusion of previously excluded constituencies. The hopes generated by the opening of traditionally closed doors cannot easily be discouraged. Demands for further involvement, access, and participation are likely to increase. Yet these demands are likely to be taken to the courts more often than to the barricades; indeed, claims to participation are already being litigated.

Early in the spring of 1970 a group of graduate teaching assistants at the University of Wisconsin filed a suit seeking to have certain departmental meetings opened to the public. The complaints asserted that a general state "open meeting" law applied even to faculty deliberations, historically closed and often confidential. At the initial hearing on the case, the judge suggested that the department hold a single public meeting to reconsider its general policy. Without awaiting further proceedings, the department accepted the suggestion, met in public, and announced that all future meetings would be open. It seems doubtful that the court would ever have required the department to go so far; yet the mere filing of suit accomplished the desired result.

Other cases recently in the courts raise comparable claims. A group of students at the State University of New York at Buffalo brought suit in the summer of 1970, contending that recently promulgated student conduct rules were invalid because the governing board failed to consult students and faculty as arguably required by state statute. A year and a half later, suit was brought in California by a faculty union, alleging that the university administration and the regents were covertly changing the procedures for nontenure appointments before consulting with faculty representatives.

In the most striking of the recent cases, a black community association in Philadelphia brought suit to challenge the dismissal of several staff members of the Temple University Community Mental Health Center. The complaint dealt specifically with the personnel matters and more broadly alleged noncompliance with federal statutes governing the use of certain funds received by the clinic. But the plaintiffs went even further, seeking a court declaration that the university had failed to give the surrounding community a voice in the "center's planning, operation, and administration." They asked the court for a "declaration that the control of the center rests with the community (in particular the plaintiff association)." The court ruled against the plaintiffs, but on the narrow ground that a similar complaint was then pending before the appropriate federal agency and that no need had been shown for early judicial intervention. In the course of the opinion, the court distinguished between community *participation* (required by federal statute and apparently assured by Temple) and community *control* (sought by the plaintiffs but not required by law). The court also remarked that since none of the plaintiffs were members of the center's staff, they apparently lacked the requisite legal standing to bring such a matter before the court.

The Temple case turns upon a special set of facts. Yet the suit does suggest that community demands for involvement in university decisions arguably affecting community interests may be increasingly channeled into the courts. Whether adequate internal forms of accommodation can be developed—for example, community representation on the new university-wide senates—remains to be seen. It is too early to predict whether courts will recognize such claims beyond the rather vague statutory mandates of "consultation" and "participation." In any event, this is an area of law to watch closely.

THE LEGAL STATUS OF PUBLIC AND PRIVATE COLLEGES

Until rather recently, courts drew sharp distinctions between public and private institutions of higher learning. Such distinctions turned almost entirely on matters of form rather than substance. Thus, Howard University, the University of Pittsburgh, and Temple University would have been held private despite their heavy dependence on public support. During the 1960s a series of cases arose in the federal courts which sharply tested that historic dichotomy—cases in which the very existence of federal jurisdiction depended upon a finding of "state action." The results varied widely, and no clear pattern emerged.

Tulane University was held to be private despite its origin as the official, public university of Louisiana; Columbia University and the University of Denver were also held private despite the receipt of massive amounts of federal funds, state and local tax benefits, and the performance of a vital public function under governmental regulation. The University of Tampa, however, was held to be public because surplus city land and buildings had made possible its early development, and the public character of Howard was implicitly recognized because of its nearly total dependence on federal funds for operation, despite its technically private charter and governing board.

The most interesting case of the 1960s involved Alfred University. A private liberal arts college in upstate New York, Alfred is the host campus for one of the State University of New York contract colleges (ceramics). Alfred provides liberal arts education to the ceramics students (roughly one-third of the student body) and grants the degrees, in return for which the state pays about one-fifth of the operating budget and the salaries of the same fraction of the faculty. When a group of Alfred students—some in ceramics and others in liberal arts—were suspended following an anti-ROTC demonstration, the nature of the institution came squarely before the federal courts. The students argued that Alfred was public for all purposes, while the university's lawyers insisted the presence of the contract college did not impair Alfred's historically private status. The court of appeals split the institution down the middle, holding that a ceramics student would be entitled to due process and all the substantive guarantees of the Bill of

Rights, while his roommate in liberal arts would not. There was a curious twist to the decision: the court found the liberal arts sector beyond the reach of the Constitution because there was insufficient "governmental involvement" in the very act complained of, the imposition of student discipline. In fact, under the agreement between Alfred and SUNY, the dean of students wore two hats—as an officer of the private campus and as an agent of the state—and a pro rata share of his salary was paid from legislative appropriations.

A subsequent New York case carried the analysis much further and qualified the Alfred holding. Wagner College, a small Lutheran institution on Staten Island, is about as "private" as one could imagine. Along with most other private colleges and universities, Wagner responded to the Henderson law in the summer of 1969 by filing a copy of its student conduct rules and disciplinary procedures in Albany. The next spring, several black students were involved in a sit-in at Wagner and were promptly dismissed; they brought suit in a federal court seeking reinstatement. The plaintiffs conceded that such a case could not have succeeded in the past, but argued that "state action" or "governmental involvement" now existed since the very rules they had violated were adopted and filed in response to a state law. The district judge dismissed the case, following the old precedents. The court of appeals remanded, however, for further study of the question. In the Alfred opinion, the court had suggested federal jurisdiction might exist "if New York had undertaken to set policy for the control of demonstrations in all private universities." It was not clear whether this had in fact been the case—whether Wagner already had its own conduct rules prior to 1970, or had drafted new rules in response to the Henderson law. In a special concurring decision, Judge Henry Friendly (author of the Alfred opinion) found the plaintiffs' claim somewhat clearer:

> The ordinary citizen must find it puzzling enough that there is a constitutional limit on the extent of state regulation of student conduct at Buffalo and Stony Brook but none at Columbia and Cornell that courts should not be adverse to recognizing state action with respect to the latter when New York has departed, even in a rather minor way, from the hands-off policy it followed until 1969.

We shall never know the outcome of the case, however, because the students were reinstated soon after the remand.

The status of private colleges and universities before the courts remains uncertain. In a few states, notably New York, the *state* courts have freely entertained such suits, though in most states only alleged breaches of contract and the like are regularly cognizable in such cases. Since it seems unlikely this situation will change, the expanding accountability already mentioned will have to occur in the federal courts. The amenability of the private institutions to suit and to the guarantees of the United States Constitution will depend partly on the degree of governmental involvement—not simply fiscal support, but regulation, control, and cooperation as well. Consistent with these criteria, a New York state trial court has held that Hofstra University—a fairly representative private institution—is subject to the federal Constitution simply because of its fiscal interdependence with the state. The court cited the extensive use of state funds to build residence halls, the number of Hofstra students receiving state and federal financial aid, the use of federal land for campus expansion, and various state and local tax exemptions which indirectly benefit the university.

The state of the law may itself change, however, so as to bring private universities under the Constitution. A persuasive case can be made, though it has never been accepted by the courts, that there really is no such thing as a private college or university. The function of providing higher education and awarding degrees is quasi-governmental in character; in other contexts the Supreme Court has held that technically private entities exercising government-like powers are bound by the Constitution. Moreover, all states exercise some control over private campuses; New York differs more in degree than in kind from the typical pattern. Finally, present levels of monetary support have already created a very substantial interdependence between government and private higher education. Apart from state and local funds, on a per student basis the private institutions of the country receive roughly twice as many federal dollars as the public campuses. It is quite possible that within the next decade courts will hold substantial monetary support alone sufficient to bind the recipient to the Bill of Rights.

LITIGATION BY INSTITUTIONS TO PROTECT THEIR OWN INTERESTS

Institutions of higher learning will be in court not only as defendants but also as plaintiffs in the coming decade. Reference was made earlier to the remarkable suit brought by the University of Michigan, and by Michigan State and Wayne State universities challenging the constitutionality of the 1970 budget conditions imposed by the legislature.

Michigan governing boards have not been alone in resorting to the courts for protection. When the Pennsylvania loan-and-scholarship law was enacted in 1970, many colleges simply refused to sign the required agreement to report criminal law and campus rule violations of Pennsylvania students. Since noncompliance rendered the institution and all Pennsylvanians enrolled there ineligible for further assistance, the pressure for relief was substantial.

The governing boards of Haverford and Goddard colleges brought a suit alleging substantial invasion of institutional and individual constitutional rights. Before the case came to trial, they were joined by thirty-one other colleges and universities as amici curiae, including Harvard, Princeton, Wayne State, Carleton, Vassar, Oberlin, and the University of San Francisco. Supporting briefs were also filed by sympathetic organizations, including the National Students Association and the American Association of University Professors. In the summer of 1971, the three-judge panel struck down the most onerous provisions of the law.

Institutions of higher learning have also begun to challenge regulation by external agencies. The University of California—technically the Golden Bear Athletic Fund—has brought suit against the National Collegiate Athletic Association seeking to have the entrance examination-disqualification rule set aside. The complaint has raised a broad range of questions about the fairness and validity of NCAA regulations and procedures. The trial court decided the case in favor of the Golden Bear Athletic Fund—and thus effectively in favor of the university and the students. Further proceedings may help to define the legal status of and constitutional limits upon NCAA—and recognize in turn the constitutional rights of institutions and individual athletes subject to association rules.

The activities of the accrediting associations have also been challenged in court. Several years ago Parsons College unsuccessfully sought review of the North Central States Association's revocation of its membership. Recently, Marjorie Webster Junior College, historically excluded as a profit-making institution, sued to gain admission to the Middle States Association. A district judge found the exclusion arbitrary and unrelated to the stated objectives of the association. The court of appeals reversed the decision, but essentially on the ground that the antitrust laws did not apply to higher education. Marjorie Webster also invoked the federal Constitution, claiming that Middle States failed to accord due process to applicants for membership. This issue was not fully explored on the appeal, because of the priority of the antitrust claim. This case reserved the important question of whether or not decisions about accreditation constitute state action. Given that eligibility for most federal programs and for the transfer of credits to other campuses is contingent upon membership, it is unlikely that these associations will remain permanently beyond the reach of the Constitution.

Perhaps most striking has been the tendency of colleges and universities to use the courts for resolution of *internal* controversies. The first evidence of this practice was the rash of requests for injunctions in the spring of 1969, at a time when a court order enforceable by contempt seemed far preferable to calling the police. When the injunction-violation cases reached the courts in the summer of 1969, certain defects began to appear and many citations were dismissed. Use of campus injunctions was further discouraged by the outcome of a case involving forty-five faculty members at SUNY-Buffalo arrested in March 1970 for a peaceful protest in the president's office. The professors were charged with both civil and criminal contempt for violating a trial court injunction issued two weeks earlier against campus violence and disorder. But the convictions were set aside by the appellate court because of several defects in the procedure. The order was in no sense directed specifically against these faculty members, nor were they ever served with it—even though copies had been posted around the campus. Nor were the defendants ever afforded an opportunity to appear and contest the validity of the injunction, since it was not addressed to them. These defects, together with certain faults in the trial court procedure, rendered the injunction unenforceable. Widespread publicity given to the Buffalo case has probably diminished the enthusiasm of university administrators and attorneys for the use of such court restraining orders.

Apart from the special shortcomings of the Buffalo injunction, the procedure is hazardous in other respects. Basically, it represents the surrender to an external tribunal of questions concerning faculty and student conduct that have historically been resolved on the campus. Resort to an injunction implies that campus machinery can no longer function. The procedures, moreover, fall short of those required in a criminal case and those usually afforded by campus tribunals. A person cited for contempt is seldom entitled to a jury trial, and the court's inquiry is typically confined to the narrow factual question whether the injunction was violated. Hence the reluctance of many campus administrators to employ the injunction is altogether understandable.

If the injunction is the most celebrated relegation of internal disputes to the courts, it is not the only one. The trustees of the California State Colleges discovered recently that the chairman of the mathematics department at Los Angeles State not only was not teaching an assigned class on his own campus, but was in fact being paid for teaching a course at a private university at the very same hour. After a hearing the professor was dismissed—the first tenured faculty member to be fired by the state colleges in some years. Not satisfied with this penalty, the trustees brought suit to recover some $82,569 from the hapless mathematician, the amount reflecting the salary he had allegedly been paid for not teaching and for which he had given undeserved workload credit to his colleagues. The function of this suit is problematic. Obviously the amount involved is relatively insignificant to the trustees. The true objective, therefore, must be to get a judicial vindication of the trustees' position and thereby to serve notice on campus administrators of the possible consequences of dereliction or sloppiness.

There are few limits upon the range of internal questions that might be brought to court. When the University of Texas regents sought to suppress the *Daily Texan*, apparently because of stories critical of the governing board, the first step was to rescind the charter of the student-run corporation that published the paper. A demand for the surrender of the paper's equipment followed but was rebuffed by the corporation's directors. The regents then filed suit in the state courts, demanding the return of property allegedly acquired through the use of student fees.

The receptivity of the courts to college-initiated suits of this kind is a mixed blessing. Judicial intervention seems appropriate to challenge the Michigan budget conditions, the Pennsylvania scholarship reporting requirement, and perhaps the discretion of NCAA and the regional accrediting agencies. Far less clear is the soundness of taking the Los Angeles mathematician and the publishers of the *Daily Texan* to court. Litigation is a two-edged sword. The more colleges and universities appear as plaintiffs in marginal matters, the readier judges will be to reject the claims of autonomy pressed by academic defendants. What is required is a clearer set of policies and priorities on the use of the courts, enforced by a self-restraint that comes hard to those who have only recently discovered the wonders of the judicial system. Unless such self-restraint is exercised, the vital internal processes and prerogatives may become increasingly difficult to protect.

DECISION-MAKING PROCEDURES

Largely as a result of forces and factors that have been traced in this paper, the American university has already become, in its administrative aspects, a quasi-judicial institution. This metamorphosis results partly from the increasingly legal nature of the most difficult internal controversies, and partly from the increasing subjection of academic decisions to the scrutiny of courts. In the process, the informal ways of past years have been discredited and repudiated—sometimes more because they are *flexible* than because they are *fallible*. (The counseling processes of the kindly old dean have been equated in the past decade with arbitrariness, haste, and selective enforcement of vague rules.) The consequences of university action, moreover, are admittedly more serious than was the case a decade or two ago as both the necessity of a college degree and the value of a baccalaureate education—especially in public institutions—have risen sharply in recent years.

Meanwhile, colleges and universities have tended to *over*judicialize —that is, they have applied formal techniques more broadly than was necessary or even wise. When student conduct codes finally caught up with standards expected of most administrative agencies, there was a tendency to overcompensate for the sloppiness and informality of the past. The presence of lawyers on campus for the resolution of one type of controversy sometimes carried over to other matters that could have been resolved more easily and less formally by laymen. The very novelty of quasi-judicial procedures has been a source of fascination for some and thus a contributor to overreliance upon formality.

All this is familiar to any observer of contemporary higher education. The important question is where things are likely to go in the decade ahead. The answer depends partly on the range of issues that reach the courts—a factor which rests in turn upon a set of considerations explored in an earlier section. There is, as has been suggested, a seemingly circular relationship between internal procedures and external constraints. The more campus tribunals do in fact observe due process and adjudicate fairly, the less they will be forced to do so by reviewing courts. Yet it is virtually certain that the range of issues potentially subject to court review will continue to expand until virtually any judgment that significantly affects the rights or interests of the campus community will be reviewable.

A second factor is either the cause or the consequence of the first, or perhaps partly both—the increasing prominence of lawyers in the general administration of higher education. The process of decision making is influenced not only by having attorneys as presidents of Harvard, Yale, Rutgers, Iowa, Case-Western Reserve, Goddard, and innumerable other campuses of all sizes and varieties. In addition, the presence and importance of lawyers in middle-level nonlegal posts appears to be increasing, with the result that legal approaches are more likely to be taken for even routine academic matters.

Third, judicialization may increase simply because the other university constituencies will more often be represented by counsel than in the past. Where collective bargaining develops, union lawyers will participate in discussion of a wide range of issues formerly settled among laymen. Student governments and organizations have increasingly retained counsel, as noted earlier. Even community organizations are more likely to come to campus with attorneys, whether or not they bring potentially justiciable grievances.

Fourth, formal procedures are likely to be mandated in a growing number of states by the application to higher education of general administrative procedure statutes—a factor mentioned earlier. Whether such procedures are appropriate to academic institutions is another, and quite difficult question. At least they tend to be sounder and more workable than ad hoc procedures drafted by laymen. General regulations of this type usually have a good deal of interpretation to guide their application. They are also more likely than local ad hoc rules to cover wholly unforeseen contingencies. Thus, despite the obvious differences, the benefits of uniformity may outweigh the risks of treating university decision making in the same manner as the internal affairs of motor vehicle bureaus or liquor licensing agencies.

Several practical suggestions emerge from this review. College and university administrators should be prepared to live with formal procedures for some time, and probably for an expanding range of issues. But they should also know where to draw the line and be prepared to do so, by insisting that formality is not required for every campus dispute. A conscientious attempt should be made to identify the areas of decision making for which formal procedures are inappropriate—and concerning which the institution would be willing to defend the fairness of its informal methods.

At least in the short run, greater centralization and clearance of certain types of decisions may be desirable to avoid potential liability and litigation. While lawyers will tend to err on the side of formality and deliberation, their instincts are more often excessively cautious than wrong.

Because of the greater visibility of all sorts of decisions—up to and including personnel judgments—standards as well as procedures will become vitally important. To paraphrase an ancient adage, universities must not only do justice in fact but be seen to do justice. Thus accountability and visibility, apart from anything else, will impose constraints both on the decision-making process and on the substantive criteria.

There are two major caveats. First, the whole corpus of higher education law has been profoundly affected by the Supreme Court decisions in the summer of 1972, involving recognition of student organizations and nonreappointment of faculty members. Basic principles of constitutional law have been announced by the Court which must be refined and applied by the lower courts over the next decade. Because the Supreme Court has spoken so seldom on these questions, its dual decisions in 1972 have vast implications for the future. The other reason for suspending or qualifying judgment is the uncertain impact of collective bargaining. While it seems unlikely that the spread of faculty unionization will greatly alter university structures, it may significantly affect the decision-making process. Union and management may contract for procedures as formal or as informal as they like, and courts are bound to respect the choice within broad limits. Thus the extent to which universities become or remain judicialized may depend, after all, on factors that await further experience.

THE UNIVERSITY AS CLIENT

Presumably the importance of lawyers *as lawyers* will continue to increase in the decade ahead. This projection has a series of specific corollaries, which are reviewed below.

First, the total budget for university legal services will probably have to expand substantially—either by hiring additional attorneys or by retaining private law firms on special assignments. Small colleges that have had modest retainers in the past may now have to engage full or part-time attorneys. In large systems, the total size of the legal staff may have to be materially increased, even in a time of scarce resources and countless other claimants. (The budgets for *security* and *police* services have been greatly enlarged in the aftermath of disorder, but as yet few positions have been added to the general counsel's office because the need for augmentation was less clear.)

Second, there must be decentralization of legal services in large systems. Local campus counsel have been provided in many systems, but in two of the largest—the University of California and the California State Colleges—the legal office remains centralized. Localization is necessary not only because problems arise and must be dealt with at the local level, often faster than the time it takes to get a lawyer from headquarters, but also because the autonomy of each campus is only as strong as the ability of its president or chancellor to make his own decisions about legal matters.

Third, greater attention should be given to the use of paraprofessionals for tasks that require some legal insight but not a professional Juris Doctor degree. The number of such tasks in even a moderately complex university far exceeds the availability of professional legal counsel. Throughout the student affairs division, in the business office, the personnel department, and in many sensitive academic areas, legal implications abound but are widely committed to persons lacking any legal expertise. Just as paraprofessional courses are being developed for legal secretaries, for prison counselors, court workers and administrators, and others, a new sort of short-term legal program should be developed for the wide range of university persons who would benefit from it.

Fourth, a special and distinct field of study should be recognized in the law of higher education. Despite the vast number of court cases, statutes, and administrative rulings involving university legal questions, there still exists hardly a course in higher education law—save for an occasional seminar offered by a harried law professor turned administrator who lacks time to teach anything else. As much as the other special fields in which law students concentrate or major in the third year, higher education is a discrete topic meriting separate attention. For lawyers already in practice, there is an urgent need for in-service or supplemental programs—along the lines of those offered by the Michigan Institute of Continuing Legal Education on student discipline law and collective bargaining in higher education. Because of the rapid and profound changes within the past five years, every university lawyer should be expected to take such a course; to counsel or represent a university without such training is rather similar to a tax lawyer, having learned the 1939 Internal Revenue Code in law school, continuing to practice without a refresher course in the 1954 code.

Fifth, separate and potentially conflicting legal interests should be recognized and represented accordingly. It is no longer the case, if it ever was, that the legal interests of the governing board, the central administration, the local campus president and the deans or department chairmen are in perfect harmony. Yet even where legal services are readily available, there is an assumption of identity of interests. When the university is sued, everyone must be represented by the general counsel (or not at all) even though the client, which is the governing board or the central administration, may have either no interest or interests potentially conflicting with those of other defendants. And if the university lawyer declines even for valid professional reasons to represent a dean or department head, there is typically no authority to go elsewhere. The time has come to dispel the notion of harmony among legal interests and recognize the complexity and potential conflicts—just as lawyers and courts recognize in other analogous contexts where separate counsel may be required to represent co-parties.

Sixth, as a corollary, provision should be made for the absorption or reimbursement of legal costs incurred in the course of official service or responsibility. Such an obligation is seldom recognized. Recently, however, the New Jersey legislature provided that when any faculty member in a state-supported college or university is sued "for any act or omission arising out of and in the course of the performance of the duties of such office," the state shall defray all costs "including reasonable counsel fees and expenses, together with the costs of appeal, if any. . . ." This seems a reasonable policy recognizing the realities and hazards of modern academic life. The New Jersey law provides a model which other states and private universities might emulate.

Finally, thought should be given to developing various forms of insurance to cover the possible consequences of legal liability. Lawyers, doctors, and many other professionals typically carry some form of "malpractice" insurance. The time may not be far off when all university officials should be similarly protected, though it is hard to imagine individual faculty members needing comparable coverage. Perhaps for the moment the issue need only be raised, with any recommendations to await further study of possible options.

INTER-INSTITUTIONAL COOPERATION

Cooperation and common cause among institutions of higher learning may be relevant to their legal posture. At the very least, there should be far more sharing of legal information and recent developments among presidents of related institutions. In 1971, for example, the Inter-University Council of Ohio (an organization including all the public campuses of the state) called upon member institutions to share with other members any requests to the state attorney general for legal advice and the results of the inquiry. Court decisions affecting one Ohio campus are distributed among the others—a practice which is less systematically followed in other states but should be formalized everywhere.

Second, there is strength in numbers when policy is being made or affected at the state or federal level. Some support for this view comes from the role of the American Council on Education (ACE) during the IRS drafting of the summer 1970 guidelines for released time for political activities; and more recently, the involvement of ACE in the wage-price freeze preliminaries. What one campus or even system could not possibly do on its own, an umbrella organization may be able to do. The potential for such comprehensive associations as ACE has not been fully realized at the national level, nor have comparable statewide higher education lobbies been maximally utilized.

Third, there is certainly a need for joinder of forces in the event of litigation. The Michigan suit was undoubtedly made more effective (and the individual costs reduced) by the willingness of Michigan State and Wayne State to join the university regents in the courts. Similarly, the federal suit challenging Pennsylvania's financial aid law was strengthened when thirty-one colleges and universities throughout the country, public and private, joined Haverford and Goddard as amici curiae. Collaborative enterprises of this sort will become more necessary as the need for and the expenses of litigation increase; even without formal consortia, ad hoc coalitions of institutions sharing a common concern about an eternal threat should be viable.

Apart from direct threats forcing institutions to come together, the potential of the law for facilitating cooperation has hardly been tested. New legal arrangements should be developed for consortia and sharing arrangements of various types, short of complete fusion or merger. Such ententes might enable neighboring institutions to share better the cost of expensive new facilities; to effect a sounder division of labor in academic policy and planning; to expand the options available to students, and the like. To date almost all of the consortia are permanent and comprehensive—like the Claremont colleges, the Connecticut River Valley alliance, and the graduate-level consortium in the District of Columbia. There may be substantial untapped potential in short-term or special-purpose arrangements to meet a particular need without sacrificing autonomy to the degree implicit in a merger or major consortium. The law can be quite helpful here.

DEFINING INSTITUTIONAL GOALS AND INTERESTS

Earlier it was suggested that departures from neutrality in admissions and employment—preferential minority group programs, for example—may depend upon a clear delineation of legitimate educational needs and interests. At another point it was predicted that courts in reviewing university sanctions will increasingly insist that the penalty must bear a direct relationship to some special interest of the institution, and not merely a widely shared interest enforced through the criminal law. The two earlier points converge here: there is a fairly urgent need for institutions not having a clear statement of goals and interests (as most do not) to develop such a list. The fullest participation of all campus constituencies should be assured in so vital and transcendent a matter—thus making the process somewhat more difficult than an administrative fiat, but the results more durable.

There is relatively little guidance in the matter of defining institutional goals. One recent study for the Carnegie Commission on Higher Education reveals that comprehensive statements of goals are comparatively rare. Many suggestions could be offered for the process of identifying and defining such goals, but that is not the task of this paper. For the moment it is enough to stress the importance of taking the necessary steps so that adequate standards will be available in the event of litigation.

The definition of institutional *interests* may be somewhat easier. In various respects colleges and universities have special claims to regulate conduct and behavior. First, the academic institution may derive certain special authority from its function as landlord—not merely because it owns buildings, but because it maintains them for special purposes, notably learning, study, and research, which may warrant a different standard of conduct from that appropriate for a bus station, airport, or hotel. Second, the university, of course, has paramount interests in preserving the integrity of its educational processes. These interests may sometimes carry campus sanctions beyond those of the general law—forbidding, for example, the reading of foreign language works in translation for language courses, though the legislature could hardly make such conduct criminal. Other special regulatory interests can be briefly noted here since they have been more fully developed elsewhere: the protection of the physical health and safety of students; the protection of the integrity of extracurricular activities from external forces such as gambling; and the responsibility of the university to the larger community. Caution is appropriate, however; the university may not justify punishment of student or faculty conduct by the need to preserve the good will of important politicians or alumni. The interests must be defined with some precision in order to avoid their abuse and to afford adequate guidance to courts called upon to review academic judgments and sanctions.

IMPROVING THE LEGAL CLIMATE

Time and again in this paper it has been suggested that judges, almost all of whom are college graduates, do not know very much about higher education. While this lack of expertise is quite understandable, it can produce fearsome results, as some of the recent New York cases suggest. Judges occasionally liken universities to factories, hospitals, and elementary or secondary schools and cannot appreciate the case for autonomy or for different standards and procedures. Short of replacing the present bench, what is to be done to improve the situation?

First, there is considerable hope for educating the courts about higher education. The Marjorie Webster accreditation case provides a valuable illustration, regardless of how one feels about the outcome.

When the district judge held higher education subject to the antitrust laws, and substituted his own judgment for that of the regional association about the proprietary standard, alarm ran through the academic community. The implications of the decision were vast. Within weeks, eleven organizations accounting for much of American higher education prepared amicus curiae briefs for the appeal. The higher court might well have held as it did in any event, but the careful and thorough explanation of the nature and needs of modern higher education doubtless reinforced the judgment that universities are not interchangeable with factories.

The same educational approach was taken in the nonrenewal cases that were recently before the Supreme Court. Although the academic community was rather sharply split on this issue, the Court received a wealth of pertinent background material to aid the understanding of a difficult and complex question. The same approach is planned by a dozen or more interested educational groups in the University of Washington preferential admissions case, where the understanding of the graduate admissions process is vital to an informed decision. This approach should be taken whenever a case of such importance reaches an appellate court, and not simply at the Supreme Court level.

Second, some thought might be given to special expert tribunals for the adjudication of higher education questions. There exist specialized courts of various sorts—a court of customs and patent appeals, a court of claims, a court of military appeals and a tax court in the federal system, and more modest tribunals at the state level. Perhaps it would not be too bold to suggest a special educational court, the members of which would be judges specially qualified and experienced in academic matters. The process of reviewing a substantial number and broad range of such cases, either at the trial or appellate level, might develop a more uniform and reliable body of precedent. Of course there are problems—as witness the substantial variations among the higher education laws of the states.

Even these variations may not, however, be immutable. Harmonization and uniformity of laws have been achieved in areas where skeptics would have thought it impossible. The adoption by forty-nine states of the Uniform Commercial Code attests vividly to the potential of assimilation. The growing acceptance—now by some twenty states—of the uniform national bar examination is another illustration of the process. Perhaps the time has come to develop a uniform national higher education act. Such a law, if adopted by many states, would greatly facilitate the transition of faculty from one system to another (by creating, for example, interchangeability in retirement and insurance systems). Uniformity might also serve to reduce the barriers to interstate migration of students, as is done to a limited degree among neighboring Big Ten campuses in the Midwest. Needless litigation might also be reduced, because the applicable law would have general rather than local force. The elimination of duplication and needless competition in many areas might reduce higher education costs and realize other benefits.

This final set of suggestions is undoubtedly unrealizable at this time. Before we begin thinking about uniform law or a special court for academic cases, much more urgent business demands our attention. But someday, when the relations between law and higher education are a bit smoother than they are just now, further study of such options may be profitable.

CED Editorial Board for Education Studies

W. D. EBERLE
Special Representative for Trade Negotiations
Executive Office of the President

HARRY W. KNIGHT
Chairman of the Board
Knight, Gladieux & Smith, Inc.

ALFRED C. NEAL
President
Committee for Economic Development

FRANK W. SCHIFF
Vice President and Chief Economist
Committee for Economic Development

ALAN K. CAMPBELL
Dean, The Maxwell School of Citizenship and Public Affairs
Syracuse University

LAWRENCE C. HOWARD
Dean, Graduate School of Public and International Affairs
University of Pittsburgh

STERLING M. McMURRIN
Dean, Graduate School
University of Utah

CED Research Advisory Board

Chairman
CARL KAYSEN
Director
The Institute for Advanced Study

EDWARD C. BANFIELD
The Fels Center
University of Pennsylvania

ALAN K. CAMPBELL
Dean, The Maxwell School of Citizenship and Public Affairs
Syracuse University

WILBUR J. COHEN
Dean, School of Education
The University of Michigan

LAWRENCE C. HOWARD
Dean, Graduate School of Public and International Affairs
University of Pittsburgh

CHARLES P. KINDLEBERGER
Department of Economics and Social Science
Massachusetts Institute of Technology

JOHN R. MEYER
President
National Bureau of Economic Research

ARTHUR OKUN
The Brookings Institution

DON K. PRICE
Dean, John Fitzgerald Kennedy School of Government
Harvard University

RAYMOND VERNON
Graduate School of Business Administration
Harvard University

MURRAY L. WEIDENBAUM
Department of Economics
Washington University

PAUL N. YLVISAKER
Dean, Graduate School of Education
Harvard University